THE EXTRAORDINARY LIFE OF

MALALA
YOUSAFZAI

Written by Hiba Noor Khan
Illustrated by Rita Petruccioli

Kane Miller
A DIVISION OF EDC PUBLISHING

Pakistan

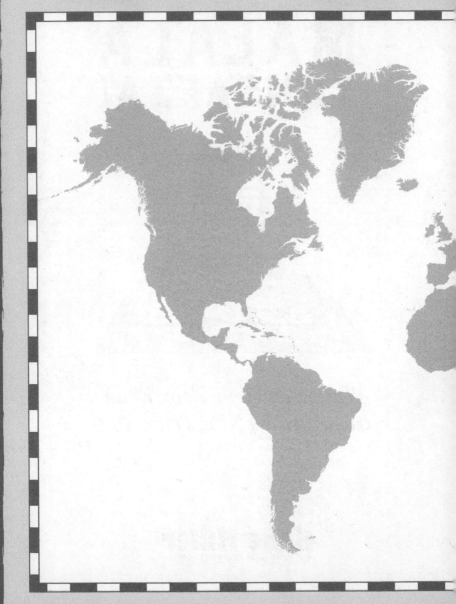

THE EXTRAORDINARY LIFE OF

MALALA
YOUSAFZAI

First American Edition 2020
Kane Miller, A Division of EDC Publishing

Original edition first published by Penguin Books Ltd, London
Text copyright © Hiba Noor Khan 2019
Illustrations copyright © Rita Petruccioli 2019
The author and the illustrator have asserted their moral rights.

For information contact:
Kane Miller, A Division of EDC Publishing
P.O. Box 470663
Tulsa, OK 74147-0663
www.kanemiller.com
www.edcpub.com
www.usbornebooksandmore.com

Library of Congress Control Number: 2019942942

Printed and bound in the United States of America
2 3 4 5 6 7 8 9 10
ISBN: 978-1-68464-076-8

KABUL

AFGHANISTAN

MINGORA

SWAT
VALLEY

ISLAMABAD
(capital)

WAZIRISTAN

PAKISTAN

PAKISTAN

WHO IS
Malala Yousafzai?

Malala Yousafzai

was born on July 12, 1997, in the beautiful
Swat Valley in the north of Pakistan.

1

Malala's father worked as a teacher and was passionate about *education*, and her mother always encouraged Malala to do well at school.

Malala *loved learning* about everything, from physics to politics, and she was almost always top of her class.

When she was young, her days were filled with *laughter*. She often played beside the spectacular waterfalls and on the hills of Swat with her friends and two younger brothers. But when a violent group of EXTREMISTS came to her valley and a war began to rage on her doorstep, *everything changed*.

EXTREMIST: someone who has taken their political or religious views to a dangerous level.

THE TALIBAN

The violent group of extremists who came to Malala's valley were a branch of the TALIBAN, *who wanted to stop women from voting, going to school and even leaving the house alone.*

Malala and her father **refused** to remain silent about the INJUSTICE they were facing. They spoke up bravely, and Malala continued to go to school *in secret*, hiding her books and wearing her normal clothes instead of her uniform every

INJUSTICE: unfair or undeserved treatment.

day. When the Pakistani army drove the Taliban out, Malala and the other girls were finally able to return to school and continue with their lives, and it wasn't long before Malala was known all over the world for **her bravery** in the face of the terror she had lived through.

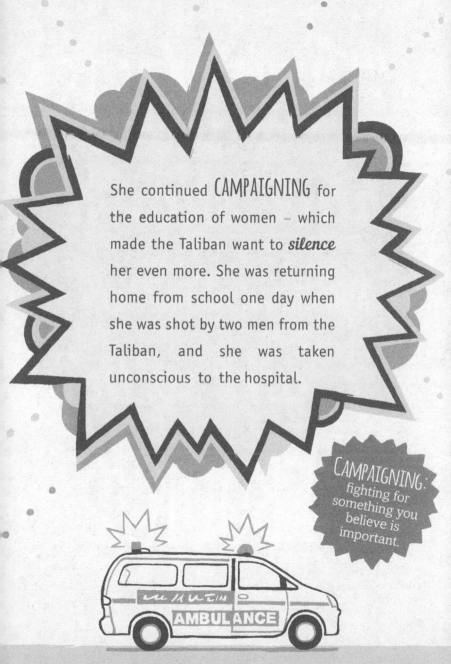

She continued CAMPAIGNING for the education of women – which made the Taliban want to *silence* her even more. She was returning home from school one day when she was shot by two men from the Taliban, and she was taken unconscious to the hospital.

CAMPAIGNING: fighting for something you believe is important.

AMBULANCE

"EXTREMISTS
have shown
WHAT FRIGHTENS THEM MOST:
a girl with
A BOOK."

– Ban Ki-moon,
former Secretary-General of the United Nations

After miraculously surviving the shooting, this *brave*, *determined* young girl went on to win the *Nobel Peace Prize*.

Malala has led an *extraordinary* life indeed – let's go back to the Swat Valley, where it all began . . .

MALALA IN THE
Swat Valley

*T*he Swat Valley in north
Pakistan, where Malala was
born and raised, is known
across the world for its
natural beauty,
and attracts many
visitors every year.

DID YOU KNOW?
Even the queen
of England has visited
the Swat Valley!

"WE LIVED IN THE MOST *beautiful place* IN ALL THE WORLD.

My valley, the Swat Valley, is a heavenly kingdom of mountains, gushing waterfalls and crystal-clear lakes."

With rivers teeming with trout, lush green fields and hills, mines glittering with emeralds and an abundance of exotic fruits, this **magical** part of the world was home to Malala and her two brothers. When she was born her family was quite poor, but they were surrounded by such **natural richness** in all the trees, mountains and vibrant colors.

Malala's namesake

In 1880, on the dusty plains of Afghanistan, a young woman named **Malalai** made history with her bravery. Her nation was at war and she stormed onto the battlefield. Her words gave *courage and strength* to the soldiers, and, though Malalai was caught up in crossfire and killed, they were *so inspired* by her passion that they fought harder and ended up winning the battle, changing the course of history.

In 1997 another Malala was born. Just like the woman she was named after, this Malala would stand up for the *justice* she believed in, reaching *millions of people* with her words.

Malala's grandfather worked as a teacher after studying in India, and had learned from observing many great leaders, including *Mahatma Gandhi* and *Muhammad Ali Jinnah*. Jinnah was renowned for his inspiring speeches, and used to give *sermons* at the mosque in their village, fascinating the villagers with world events, history and stories from the *Quran*. Malala's grandfather loved poetry, and spoke Persian and Arabic as well as their native language, *Pashto*. He was sometimes a harsh man, with very high standards, and Malala's father was always trying to make him proud.

MAHATMA GANDHI *peacefully protested against the harsh British rule of India.*

MUHAMMAD ALI JINNAH *was a leader of Pakistan who had great visions for a peaceful and harmonious country.*

Malala's father

When he was young, **Ziauddin Yousafzai**, Malala's father, was teased by other children because he had darker skin and was shorter than them. He had a **bad stutter** and struggled to get his words out, which made him very self-conscious. Ziauddin desperately wanted to please his father (who was very hard to please). One day, despite his stutter, Ziauddin decided to enter a public speaking competition. After much hard work – he didn't have the luxury of electricity in his village and had no choice but to study by the light of an oil lamp – he ended up winning *first prize*!

Ziauddin was beyond pleased when he saw his father clapping and beaming with pride at his victory. But, most importantly, he had learned how to turn what he thought was a weakness into a *strength*. He continued to work hard at school and grew up to be a very kind, generous and determined man.

Malala's mother

Malala's mother's name is *Toor Pekai* and, like lots of other girls in the Swat Valley, she didn't go to school for very long.

Did you know?
In Pashto "Toor Pekai" means "black hair," even though Malala's mother's hair is brown!

Toor Pekai's father encouraged her to attend school, but she was the *only girl* in her class. She saw all her female cousins playing and having fun at home – which made her reluctant to go to school. She secretly sold her books and used the money to buy sweets! She was naturally bright, but it was only later, when she met Ziauddin, that she began to wish she'd stuck with her *education*.

Malala's parents met through relatives and there was an *instant connection*. It took nine months for Ziauddin to persuade Toor Pekai's father to allow them to marry! Ziauddin wrote Toor Pekai romantic poems and letters – how she wished she could read and respond to them! Ziauddin believed that *education and knowledge* would solve all the problems in Pakistan and he desperately wanted to start up his own school. Toor Pekai was ready to do whatever it took to help him achieve his dream.

Although she could not recognize letters and numbers, she possessed great wisdom, strength and kindness.

"SHE IS A GREAT
person,
AND SHE HAS NOT JUST
a face of
beauty
BUT BEAUTY OF HEART."

– Malala about her mother

For years Ziauddin worked *tirelessly* to set up his school. What he lacked in money and influential contacts he made up for in drive and determination, and eventually he found somewhere and began looking for students.

The school was named the **Khushal School**, after a great Pashtun warrior.

Life in Mingora

Once they were married, Toor Pekai joined Ziauddin at the school in *Mingora*. She was excited to move to somewhere bigger and busier, but life wasn't easy. They struggled to keep the school running and feed themselves. One year the whole place was almost completely destroyed in a terrible *flash flood*. Through the difficult times their love kept them strong and they continued to work as a team.

Malala was born on July 12, 1997. Ziauddin loved his daughter so much that he wrote poems and *sang songs* about her and Malalai, her namesake. His school now had about a hundred pupils and six teachers, and Malala and her parents lived above the classrooms.

Malala's father still cleaned the floors, painted the walls and mended anything that broke.

Did you know?
Even though Ziauddin was terrified of heights he would still climb up electricity poles to hang banners advertising the school.

As soon as Malala was able to walk, the school became her *playground* and she would toddle in and out of the classrooms. The family still had hardly any money left over for themselves – they couldn't even afford milk to put in their chai. However, over the next few years, slowly but surely, more and more students signed up and life became easier. As Malala's parents saw what had once been a pipe dream grow from strength to strength, they dared to think of opening a second school, which would be named the *Malala Education Academy*.

DID YOU KNOW?

Malala's favorite colors are purple and pink, and she loves the singer Justin Bieber!

Baby Khushal was born into the Yousafzai family when Malala was two, and five years later another boy, *Atal*, came along. Compared to most other *Swati* families, who usually had seven or maybe even eight children, Malala's was considered small.

They moved their home to a building with a large flat roof where, in the evenings, Ziauddin and his friends would **congregate** to drink chai and have conversations. Curious and intelligent from a young age, Malala enjoyed sitting with them and **listening** to the chirping of the crickets as the stars brightened and the sunlight faded.

The spacious roof was also Malala's favorite place for **daydreaming**.

The roof had a perfect view of the magnificent *mountains* not far from their town. The tallest was called Mount Elum, which was shaped like a pyramid and reached up so high that the clouds danced around its peak.

Malala's house was in an area of Mingora that is known by two names: *Gulkada* and *Butkara*.

Gulkada MEANS "PLACE OF FLOWERS."
Butkara MEANS "PLACE OF BUDDHIST STATUES."

Although Pashtun people who live in the Swat Valley are Muslims, in ancient times it was home to Buddhists, so there are the remains of *Buddhist temples* near Malala's home – along with *statues* of lions and people, and even hundreds of umbrellas! Having a grand open-air museum in their backyard made games of hide-and-seek for Malala and her brothers particularly exciting.

As Malala grew up, her home was filled with *love and laughter*, and she had an especially *strong bond* with her father. He was the one she would turn to when she was upset or confused.

"*Malala* WILL BE *free* AS A *bird.*"

– Ziauddin Yousafzai

She and her family looked forward to spending the EID FESTIVALS back in her grandparents' village. They would dress in their nicest clothes, and pack gifts of rose and pistachio sweets, patterned shawls and medicine from Mingora for their relatives.

There are two religious Eid festivals each year, when people dress up and eat special food after praying in the mosque.

EID AL-FITR
celebrates the end of Ramadan.

EID AL-ADHA
is also called the "Feast of Sacrifice."

Malala and her brothers would fight to sit by the dusty windows in the colorful, intricately painted minibus that took them to the village.

They would drive through lush, fragrant paddy fields and apricot orchards before braving the narrow, mountainous dirt roads. They went *so high* that their ears would pop! Malala loved the raw natural beauty of her grandparents' village, the rich smell of soil, the bees' hives with their gloopy honey that hung from the walnut trees, the big buffaloes and bright butterflies.

Changes on the horizon

While Malala admired many parts of Pashtun culture, like generosity to guests, bravery, and caring for neighbors, deep in her heart she knew that some things needed to *change*. Just like her father, she believed that both men and women deserved an education and access to the same opportunities.

Malala had heard of the *Taliban* in neighboring Afghanistan; she knew they were a group of men who, in many instances, had misunderstood and misrepresented the *Islamic faith* and were burning down girls' schools. She was relieved that her valley was safe and that she could go to school freely.

But, even before the arrival of the Taliban, not everything in Swat was perfect. There was no trash collection, so people dumped their waste in a heap, which **grew and grew** until it was as large as a mountain. As you might expect, it smelled foul – Malala *hated* having to dispose of the family's trash!

One day she was swatting away flies and trying not to breathe through her nose when she saw something move. She was startled to see that it was a girl of about her age, with filthy matted hair and dirty scarred skin, sorting **trash** into piles before putting it into sacks. Malala was disturbed and upset to learn that many children fished **metal** out of the trash heap in order to sell it for a few rupees.

Malala's favorite TV show featured a boy with a *magic pencil* with the power to make things real. If the boy drew an apple or a cat, it would appear magically. He would use the pencil to help other people, and each night Malala prayed to God for a magic pencil of her own.

Did you know?
Malala has published a children's book called *Malala's Magic Pencil.*

She badly wanted to help people and make everyone happy. If her *prayer* was ever answered, she
decided that the children picking through the trash
mountain would be the first she would help.

THE WAR BEGINS

When Malala was just *four years old*, across the world in New York City, the terrible events of September 11, 2001, took place. The Islamic terrorist group al-Qaeda hijacked planes and crashed them into the World Trade Center, killing and injuring thousands of *innocent people*. Malala was half a world away and too young to understand what was happening, but war and violence were on their way to her peaceful valley.

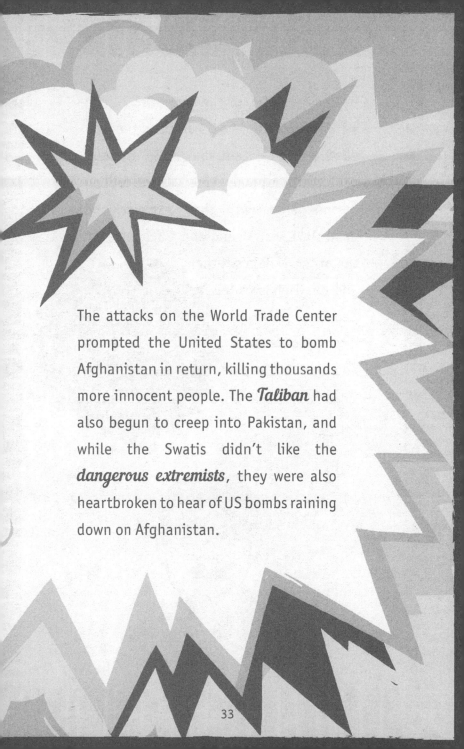

The attacks on the World Trade Center prompted the United States to bomb Afghanistan in return, killing thousands more innocent people. The *Taliban* had also begun to creep into Pakistan, and while the Swatis didn't like the *dangerous extremists*, they were also heartbroken to hear of US bombs raining down on Afghanistan.

By 2004 support for the extremist Taliban was growing, and the US dropped the first *missile* on Pakistani soil. Many ordinary people felt trapped: there was the Taliban on one side, with their extreme and OPPRESSIVE views, and the US bombs on the other. Malala's father and his friends called people together for a *peace conference*, and over 150 people turned up.

OPPRESSION: long-term cruel or unjust treatment by someone who is using their power to limit other people's freedom.

"IT'S COMING HERE. *The fire* IS REACHING THE VALLEY. *Let's put out the flames* OF MILITANCY BEFORE THEY REACH HERE."

– Ziauddin Yousafzai

MILITANCY:
the use of forceful or violent methods in support of a cause.

THE ARRIVAL OF THE TALIBAN

Malala was ten years old when a branch of the Taliban arrived in the Swat Valley. The Taliban and their leader, Fazlullah, managed to *gain support* by saying that they would help the poor and address the government's CORRUPTION.

CORRUPTION: dishonesty by someone in power, often a government.

Many villagers also saw the Taliban as saviors in the aftermath of an *earthquake* that devastated the region in October 2005.

The quake was one of the worst in history. Malala and her friends set about *fundraising* to help survivors. Aid also began pouring in from other countries' governments, but as the areas affected were often rural and very remote, it was *difficult* to land helicopters to deliver the food and supplies. In the end, much of the food and medical help delivered was from local religious organizations, some of which were branches of the Taliban.

AID
FLOUR

But the Taliban were claiming that women should stay at home, be silent, subdued and say goodbye to education. They said that this was written in the Quran, but Ziauddin told his family to *ignore* their nonsense.

In fact, the **Prophet Mohammed's** first wife, **Khadija**, was a powerful businesswoman. The Prophet Mohammed respected and honored her until she passed away. When Malala learned about Khadija at school, she thought of her own *grandmother* who, like many Pashtun women, was powerful and *strong*, raising eight children on her own while her husband was bedridden.

Misinterpretation

Part of the problem was that many Pakistanis couldn't understand *Arabic*, the language of the Quran. Men like Fazlullah took advantage of their ignorance and twisted the words to mean whatever they wanted. These so-called "religious leaders" would either *mistranslate* parts of the scripture or sometimes even make things up! This made it difficult to speak out against the Taliban.

As time went on, the Taliban became more vocal in their opinion that girls should not attend school. Almost no one had a television, so they spread their message through a *radio station*. Many people were taken in by their words.

Some of the teachers at Ziauddin's schools began obeying the Taliban and *refused* to teach girls, and many female students stopped attending altogether because they were scared of angering Fazlullah. He *insulted* girls like Malala who continued to go to school.

Malala had to hide her uniform and books in her bag, keep her head down and pray that no one stopped her as she walked to school and back.

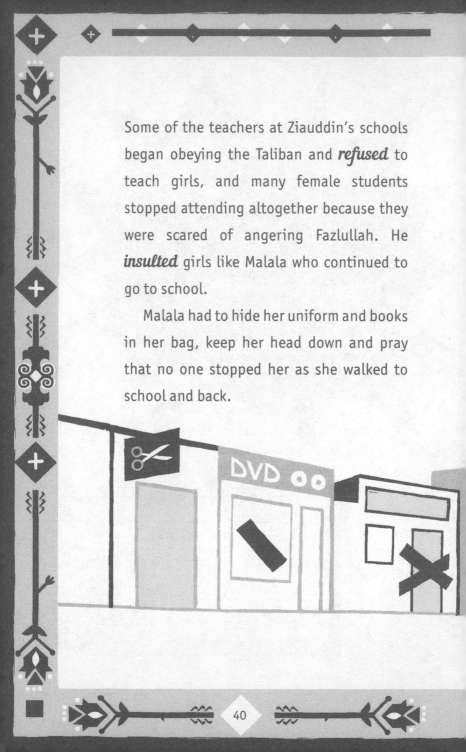

The Taliban shut down DVD shops, bazaars and barbers, stopping people from going about their normal lives, and sent out men with guns to patrol the streets. Eventually they became even more *aggressive* and began to launch attacks and bombs. The valley was fast becoming a battlefield for both the US and the Taliban.

LIFE UNDER
THE TALIBAN

*M*any popular games were **banned**, Malala's favorite TV channels were blocked, and women were **punished** if they were seen outside without a burqa. Even school trips were no longer allowed, and much of the rich culture, history and art of the valley was destroyed. The Taliban began selling the beautiful emeralds found in the mountains to buy more guns. The black clouds of **war** hung over the beautiful Swat Valley.

BANNED!

"We felt like
THE TALIBAN
SAW US AS
little dolls
TO CONTROL,
TELLING US WHAT TO DO
and how to dress."

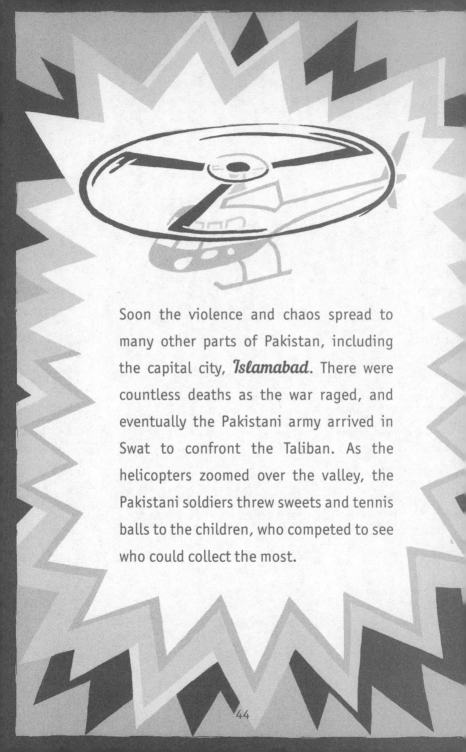

Soon the violence and chaos spread to many other parts of Pakistan, including the capital city, *Islamabad*. There were countless deaths as the war raged, and eventually the Pakistani army arrived in Swat to confront the Taliban. As the helicopters zoomed over the valley, the Pakistani soldiers threw sweets and tennis balls to the children, who competed to see who could collect the most.

The government was desperate to restore some *order* to the country. A politician named Benazir Bhutto returned to Pakistan to bring hope to the people.

Did you know?

Benazir Bhutto was the first female leader of a Muslim country in modern history. She was prime minister from 1988 to 1990, and again from 1993 to 1996.

Crowds traveled from far and wide to see her, releasing **white doves** as symbols of peace and hope.

But there were many attempts to kill her, and not long after she returned to Pakistan she was ASSASSINATED. Some said the government was responsible and some said it was the Taliban.

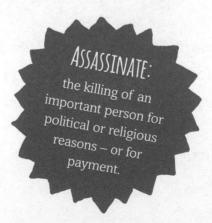

ASSASSINATE: the killing of an important person for political or religious reasons – or for payment.

"IT FELT AS IF *my country* WAS RUNNING OUT *of hope.*"

Gone were the days of dreaming on rooftops and splashing in waterfalls. The only *consolation* Malala had was school.

She was now in high school and her class was known as the "clever class" because the pupils never stopped asking questions! They were so ***passionate*** about their studies that on special occasions, instead of the traditional *mehndi* patterns of flowers and butterflies, Malala and her friends would paint chemical and mathematical ***equations*** on their hands.

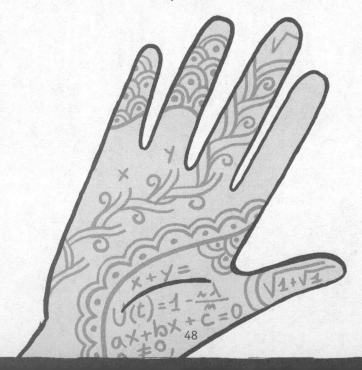

Malala worked very hard at school, and she and her best friend, Moniba, were almost always *top of the class*. In those dark and dangerous days school  was an escape, a place to laugh and forget about the worries of the world.

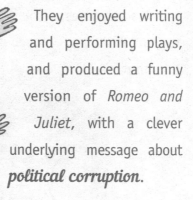 They enjoyed writing and performing plays, and produced a funny version of *Romeo and Juliet*, with a clever underlying message about *political corruption*.

Outside, the **bombs** were still falling like rain, and a couple of times they fell so close to the Yousafzai house that Malala felt the whole kitchen shake.

Malala's father and his friends understood the importance of *speaking out* against what was happening, and they began giving interviews to raise awareness. Malala also began to talk to journalists and enjoyed being able to speak her mind.

"THE
TALIBAN
are
ABUSING
our
religion."

NO MORE SCHOOL

*T*hen the Taliban announced that there would soon be a **complete ban** on girls attending school. Now life seemed even more bleak for Malala – school was her SANCTUARY. Every day it seemed that things couldn't get any worse, yet each new dawn seemed to bring more and more **bad news**.

SANCTUARY: a place to feel safe and happy.

More and more people began to understand how **terrible** the Taliban were, but they were still too **scared** to speak out against them.

Many children began to play "Army vs Taliban" rather than normal games like hide-and-seek. There were often *sleepless nights* filled with the thuds and booms of cannons and guns, and when Malala and her brothers did fall asleep they would wake up reeling from terrible nightmares.

"WHEN
someone
TAKES AWAY
your pens
YOU REALIZE QUITE
HOW IMPORTANT
education is."

> *Even as everything around her was falling apart, Malala remained strong and continued to speak up for what she believed.*

Malala carried on speaking to the media. Soon the British Broadcasting Corporation (BBC) asked her to **write a blog** about her experiences in the Swat Valley under the Taliban. Many people all over the world read her story.

In the beginning she had to use a fake name and work like a spy, writing her pieces and **secretly** giving them to a reporter, who emailed them to the BBC.

Malala understood the **power** of words, and was keen to tell her story. By the start of 2009 only ten girls remained in Malala's class. And then the day of the ban arrived. A special *assembly* was held, and everyone was emotional when the last bell rang.

When she got home that day, Malala cried and cried, feeling as if she had lost everything. She took every opportunity to give *interviews* and appear on news shows, informing the world about the *struggles* of her country. Many people told her to be careful because the Taliban would go after her for criticizing them. But she felt sure they wouldn't kill a child.

A few months later the *fighting* grew even worse: the army announced that they were going to clear the city of Mingora to drive the Taliban out. Everyone was ordered to leave immediately.

Malala's family were devastated. The Swat Valley was all they'd ever known. They packed only their most *essential belongings* and bundled into their neighbor's car.

Thousands of people were flooding out of Swat, crying and praying for a safe return, many of them with nothing but the clothes on their backs. Malala and her family struggled through *crowded roads* and checkpoints toward the village of Shangla to stay with cousins.

Home

Malala's family moved to four different towns in two months, and although it was tough they knew that they were the *lucky* ones. Thousands of others had been forced to stay in crowded *refugee camps* with little food or water.

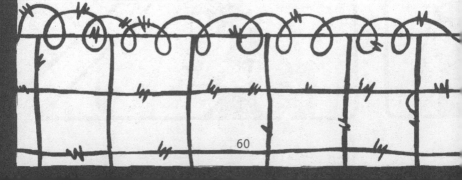

While they were away Malala turned *twelve*, but everyone was too anxious to remember her birthday. How different her eleventh birthday had been, with balloons and cake, and celebrated with friends at home. Though she was far away from that now, her *birthday wish* remained exactly the same:

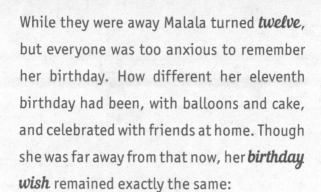

she
SIMPLY WANTED
peace.

DID YOU KNOW?

When Malala was thirteen, she also prayed to God each night to make her taller.

As soon as they heard that the fighting was over and it was *safe* to go home, they made the journey back, driving through *unrecognizable* streets.

Buildings had had their roofs and walls blown out – many were reduced to *piles of rubble* and twisted metal.

Everyone joined together for a big cleanup, and finally the *school* opened again. This was the most wonderful news for all the children, and there were tears of gratitude and hugs all around as the girls were *reunited* after what had felt like years.

However, the **army** was still everywhere and, although the Taliban had largely **disappeared**, Fazlullah was still free.

> *Many people worried that the Taliban were hiding in the mountains, just waiting to return.*

The shops reopened and women walked freely in the streets again, but the Swat Valley was not the same as it had once been as most families had had someone they loved die in the **chaos**.

Many of the trees surrounding the valley had been chopped down, disrupting the ECOSYSTEM completely.

In 2010 floods *devastated* the area, killing thousands and cutting off food supplies for Malala and her family.

ECOSYSTEM:
all the living things in a particular area and their environment, i.e. the animals, plants, water, sun, soil and climate.

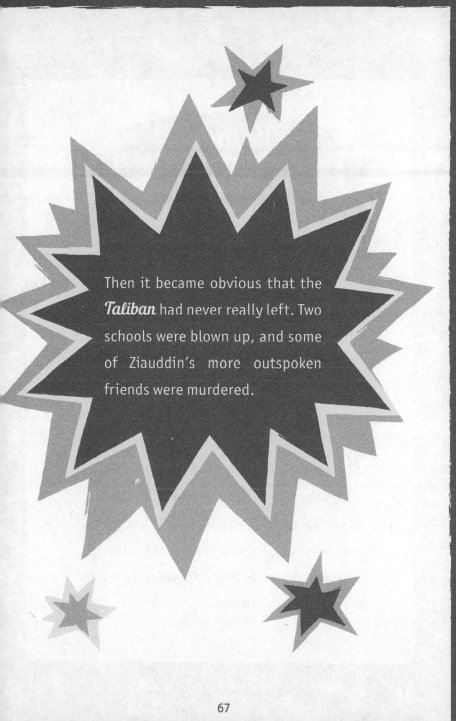

Then it became obvious that the *Taliban* had never really left. Two schools were blown up, and some of Ziauddin's more outspoken friends were murdered.

Malala's
VOICE

By now, Malala's BBC blog was *famous* across the world. Almost every day she was receiving requests to speak on TV and radio. She was also given *countless awards* because of her bravery in refusing to be silenced by the Taliban.

"WHEN THE
whole world
IS SILENT,
even one voice
BECOMES
powerful."

Schools in Pakistan were named after her, and she won Pakistan's National Youth Peace Prize, along with a great deal of money.

DID YOU KNOW?

The National Youth Peace Prize was later renamed the National Malala Peace Prize!

Malala spent much of this money on helping the needy. She *donated* large amounts to street children and schools, and began attending important *conferences*, where she argued – often successfully – for more money to be given to these causes.

Malala was regularly traveling to different cities to attend events and receive awards – but, although it was nice to be recognized, she never forgot that her goal was to bring **education and equality** to girls around the world, and she would not stop till she reached it. Malala and her father had become the face of Pakistani resistance against the Taliban; everyone knew who they were. Including their enemies.

Malala
IN DANGER

When Malala was almost fifteen, the Taliban posted an *online video* saying that they wanted her dead. Malala's parents were worried, but Malala remained calm.

"I say I AM STRONGER than FEAR."

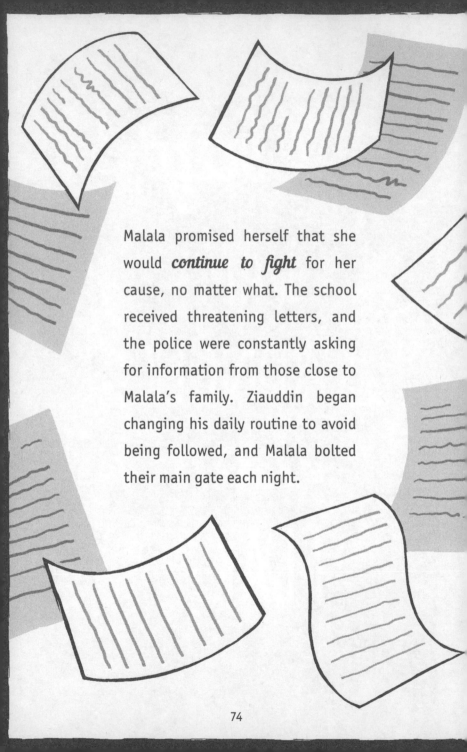

Malala promised herself that she would **continue to fight** for her cause, no matter what. The school received threatening letters, and the police were constantly asking for information from those close to Malala's family. Ziauddin began changing his daily routine to avoid being followed, and Malala bolted their main gate each night.

In October 2012, it was time for *exams* at Khushal School, and Malala had been studying (and praying!) more than usual.

The night before her first exam, Malala stayed up till 3 a.m. and reread an entire textbook!

One afternoon, she boarded the school bus with her friends, discussing the exam questions. It was a hot and humid day.

But then two young men appeared, and everything changed.

They leaned into the bus and wanted to know which girl was Malala.

When they found her, they shot her. She was unconscious before she reached the hospital.

Malala
SAVED

Over the next few days doctors struggled to save Malala's life. She and her father were flown in a helicopter to *Peshawar*. In the days after the attack, Malala's father made plans for her funeral as he didn't know if she would make it. When she did, he said that it was a *miracle*.

Malala had been shot in the head, and her brain was swelling up quickly, but after surgery lasting many hours the doctors were optimistic.

DID YOU KNOW?

Pakistani politicians offered to pay for Malala's hospital treatment.

"I DON'T WANT TO BE
REMEMBERED AS THE GIRL
who was shot.
I WANT TO BE
REMEMBERED AS THE GIRL
who stood up."

Malala still needed lots of care, and she was taken to a hospital in Birmingham, England, which specialized in *war injuries*. The prince of the United Arab Emirates supplied his personal jet to fly her to England, where she began to *recover*.

BIRMINGHAM

After a few weeks her family were given **passports** and joined her. It was three months before she was well enough to leave the hospital, and many more months of PHYSIOTHERAPY and treatment before she could see, hear, smile and walk properly again.

PHYSIOTHERAPY: the treatment of injury using massages and exercise.

DID YOU KNOW?

The staff at the hospital brought her food from KFC to cheer her up!

LIFE AFTER RECOVERY

Malala's family came to live in Birmingham, but they ***never stopped*** fighting for what they believed in.

At her new school Malala was once again a straight-A student – and here she didn't have to worry about anything other than her marks!

DID YOU KNOW?

Malala's brother Atal loves Nutella, which he discovered when the family moved to England.

The news of Malala's shooting spread fast *across the globe*, and she received thousands of get-well cards and gifts from people from many different countries. Benazir Bhutto's children sent her two of their mother's shawls, one of which Malala wore when

delivering a speech at the United Nations in New York.

Did you know?
The day Malala spoke at the United Nations was her sixteenth birthday!

"THEY THOUGHT THAT THE *bullets would silence us*, BUT THEY FAILED. AND OUT OF THAT SILENCE *came thousands of voices*."

When the family traveled to New York, Atal asked Malala what she had done to become so *famous*. He was much more interested in the Statue of Liberty and his new video game than her speech!

The Taliban had wanted to silence Malala, but the shooting had had the opposite effect. Now Malala had *support* and understanding from people all over the world.

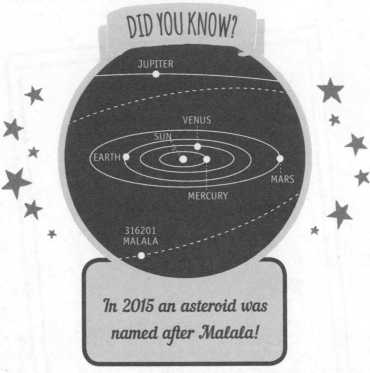

DID YOU KNOW?

JUPITER

VENUS

SUN

EARTH

MARS

MERCURY

316201
MALALA

In 2015 an asteroid was named after Malala!

Malala remembered how, many years ago, she had prayed to grow taller. She realized that, although she hadn't grown, she felt as **tall as the sky**. So tall that she couldn't even measure herself.

Malala's walls are covered with awards for **bravery** that she has received from around the world.

Did you know?
Malala is the youngest person ever to win the Nobel Peace Prize.

"ONE CHILD,
one teacher,
ONE BOOK
and one pen
CAN CHANGE
the world."

Malala's LEGACY

Malala donated all her prize money from the Nobel Prize – half a million dollars! – to the *Malala Fund*, a charity she set up to help female education projects around the world. Each year, on her birthday, she goes to meet and work with other girls who are struggling. She spent her *seventeenth birthday* in Nigeria with victims of Boko Haram, her *eighteenth* opening a school for Syrian girls in refugee camps, and her *nineteenth* with vulnerable girls in Rwanda and Kenya.

After school she went on to study *Politics, Philosophy and Economics* at the University of Oxford, where she balanced her studies with fighting for girls' education across the globe.

Sometimes Malala has flashbacks to the day of the shooting, and sometimes she feels anxious and scared, but, in the spirit of Malalai, whom she was named after, she continues to shout at the top of her lungs and from the bottom of her heart.

For it is not an army that her words will inspire, but a force far more powerful: the women of the world.

"I AM THOSE
sixty-six million girls
WHO ARE DEPRIVED
OF EDUCATION.

AND TODAY I'M NOT RAISING **MY** VOICE; *it is the voice of those sixty-six million girls."*

TIMELINE

August 14, 1947

India is split into East Pakistan (later Bangladesh), West Pakistan and India. Pakistan was created as the first-ever homeland for Muslims.

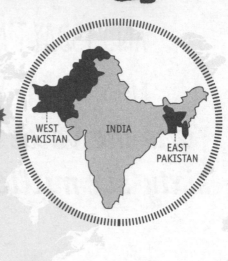

WEST PAKISTAN

INDIA

EAST PAKISTAN

1989

Soviet troops withdraw from Afghanistan following an invasion and war.

1996

Afghan Taliban take control of the capital of Afghanistan, Kabul.

2004
US begins to bomb
northwest Pakistan
using drones.

July 12, 1997
Malala is born in
the Swat Valley.

September 11, 2001
Attacks on the World Trade
Center in New York. US bombing
of Afghanistan begins.

2005

Fazlullah and the Pakistani Taliban begin preaching in the Swat Valley, insisting that girls should not go to school.

2008

Malala, age eleven, delivers her first speech against the Taliban in Peshawar.

2009

Fazlullah announces a ban on girls' schools, but Malala continues to attend in secret.

May 2009

The Pakistani army is sent to the Swat Valley to clear out the Taliban. Malala and her family leave to stay with relatives.

January 3, 2009

Using the name Gul Makai, Malala begins blogging for the BBC about her experiences as a schoolgirl under the Taliban.

July 2009

Once the Taliban have been defeated, Malala and her family return home and she attends school and goes out freely.

2010

Malala becomes more and more famous because of the BBC blog. She continues to speak and fight for education.

October 2011

Malala is nominated for the International Children's Peace Prize at age fourteen.

December 2011

Malala wins Pakistan's
National Youth Peace Prize.

October 9, 2012

On her way home after an exam, fifteen-year-
old Malala is shot by two men from the Taliban.
Two of her friends are also injured. Malala is
flown to a hospital in Birmingham, England,
where she begins to recover.

October 15, 2012

"I Am Malala" petition launched, aiming to get every child in school by 2015.

July 12, 2013

On her sixteenth birthday Malala speaks at the United Nations.

October 2013

Malala releases her autobiography, *I am Malala: The Girl Who Stood Up for Education and Was Shot by the Taliban*, and establishes the Malala Fund.

2015

Malala continues to work hard for the Malala Fund, traveling to different countries around the world to help children to access education.

October 2014

Malala is awarded the Nobel Peace Prize.

2017

Malala begins studying Politics, Philosophy and Economics at the University of Oxford.

Can you imagine how it would feel if your right to an education was taken away? How do you think Malala felt to be told that she wasn't allowed to go to school just because she was a girl?

Malala has made some amazing speeches talking about the importance of education across the world. Have you ever seen one of her speeches? Try and find one online to watch.

Malala's life so far has been full of lots of joys, but also lots of hardships – from having to leave her home, to studying in secret, to spending time in the hospital after being shot. Can you think of some characteristics that Malala has that helped her to be such a positive influence on the world?

Think about someone you really admire. Anyone – real or fictional! Can you make a list of their characteristics? Think about the aspects of their personality that make them special.

Malala is really passionate about education – she loves to learn and thinks that everyone should have the opportunity to do so. Can you think of something that you're really passionate about? It could be a subject at school, a creative skill – or a hobby that you really enjoy. What do you love about it? Do you think everyone should have the opportunity to experience it if they want to?

MORE ABOUT THE TALIBAN

*T*he Taliban have their roots in the long war that took place between the Soviet Union and the US that lasted from 1947 until 1991 – the Cold War. In the 1980s the US gave money to Pashtuns to fight against the Soviets, who had just invaded Afghanistan at the end of 1979. Some of these fighters went on to form a strict religious group that ruled much of Afghanistan.

At first they were supported by the US and by other foreign governments who saw that they were restoring order. But before long the group started to break up; many of the fighters held extreme views and became more and more corrupt. Some of them were very violent, twisting Islamic teachings beyond recognition. The Pakistani Taliban were an example of this – the group that entered the Swat Valley and caused chaos across the country were ruthless and brutal.

Most Muslims around the world CONDEMN the behavior of groups like the Taliban – they know that the Prophet Mohammed was a kind and merciful man who gave women rights rather than taking them away.

CONDEMN: express strong disapproval.

Index

Quote Sources

Direct quotes throughout are from Malala's autobiography, *I Am Malala: The Girl Who Stood Up for Education and Was Shot by the Taliban* by Malala Yousafzai and Christina Lamb, (Little Brown and Company, 2013), except the below:

Page 6: "Malala Comes to the United Nations" (Ban Ki-moon, *Huffington Post*, August 7, 2013)

Page 15: "Pizza-loving, double jointed and scared of her teachers: Meet the real Malala" (*Telegraph* article by Louise Carpenter, October 17, 2015)

Page 73: "Malala Empowers Others With #Strongerthan Social Media Campaign" (*ABC News* article by Amy Robach, July 14, 2014)

Pages 84, 88: Malala's speech to the United Nations on July 12, 2013

Pages 92, 93: Malala's Nobel Prize acceptance speech on December 10, 2014

Have you read about all of these extraordinary people?